Books by William Meredith

Hazard, the Painter   *1975*
Earth Walk: New and Selected Poems   *1970*
The Wreck of the Thresher and Other Poems   *1964*
The Open Sea and Other Poems   *1958*
Ships and Other Figures   *1948*
Love Letter from an Impossible Land   *1944*

Translated by William Meredith

Alcools: Poems 1898–1913 by Guillaume Apollinaire   *1964*

Edited by William Meredith

Shelley: Selected Poems   *1962*

Hazard, the Painter

William
Meredith

Hazard,
the Painter

Alfred A. Knopf
New York 1975

This is a Borzoi Book published by Alfred A. Knopf, Inc.
Copyright © 1972, 1973, 1974, 1975 by William Meredith
All rights reserved under International and Pan-American
Copyright Conventions. Published in the United States by
Alfred A. Knopf, Inc., New York, and simultaneously in Canada
by Random House of Canada Limited, Toronto.
Distributed by Random House, Inc., New York.

Library of Congress Cataloging in Publication Data
Meredith, William, [date]   Hazard, the painter.
I. Title.   PS3525.E588H3   811'.5'4   74-21324
ISBN 0-394-49634-5

Manufactured in the United States of America
First Edition

"Squire Hazard Walks" and "The Ghosts of the House"
originally appeared in the *New York Quarterly*.
"Music" first appeared in *Musical Newsletter*.
"Look at Me! Look at Me!" first appeared in *Shenandoah*.
"Hazard Faces a Sunday in the Decline," "Hazard's Optimism,"
"Wholesome," "Politics," and "Where He's Staying Now"
originally appeared in *Ironwood*. "Nixon's the One"
first appeared in *Inlet*.
"At the Natural History Museum" first appeared
in *Virginia Quarterly Review*.
"Nausea" and "Winter: He Shapes Up" first appeared
in *Atlantic Monthly*.
"February 14" was first published in *Georgia Review*.
"His Plans for Old Age" and "Rhode Island" were first
published in *The Hudson Review*.

In his snail-like progress through this
characterization—political references in the
poem date it like the annual rings of a weed-
tree—the author was grateful for time
provided by a grant from the National
Endowment for the Arts.

Resemblances between the life and character
of Hazard and those of the author are not
disclaimed but are much fewer than
the author would like.

for Richard Harteis

Contents

Hazard, the Painter

Hazard
Faces a Sunday
in the Decline

We need the ceremony of one another,
    meals *served,* more love,
    more handling of one another with love, less
    casting out of those who are not
    of our own household.

    'This turkey is either not cooked
    enough or it's tough.'

The culture is in late imperial decline.
    The children don't like dark meat or
    pepper. They say the mother sometimes
    deliberately puts pepper on the things
    the grown-ups like better.

    less casting out of those in our own
    household with whom we disagree.

The cat will not hear of cat-food,
    he waves it away. He has seen
    the big thrush taken from the cold
    box, dressed and put in the hot.

    'If I set the alarm-clock, will you turn
    on the oven when it goes off?' then
    she went off to see the profane
    dancers of the afternoon. It was done.

The fact that I don't like his pictures
    should not obscure the facts
    that he is a good man
    that many admire his work (his canvases
    threaten my existence and I hope
    mine his, the intolerant bastard)
    that we are brothers in humanity
    & the art. Often it does, though.

The cat has followed Hazard from his studio,
    he looks mean. He would put more pepper
    in the gravy if he knew how, he
    upbraids the innocent dog and
    all of us, he casts us out.

    'There's *pepper* in this gravy. We're
    supposed to eat dry turkey and you've
    put pepper in the gravy.'

The meal is *served,* nevertheless
    with felt love, some godless benediction.

The grown ones have wine after the other
    bottle. They cast out a lot. 'The dancers
    this afternoon were, well, *thinky,*'
    she says. She toys with her glass.

'He is strictly a one-joke painter,'
    he replies, 'painted that one twenty
    years ago and is still putting pepper
    on it, ha hah. Finish your turkey
    you two and leave a little gravy for someone else.'

The cat is taking notes against
    his own household. He watches.
    Hazard would like once to see
    things with the cat's eyes, flat.

Now it is time to go to bed. Hungry
    and alone most go to bed in this
    decline and in all others, yet

Someone has fed us again and blessed us
    with the manners of bohemia. Among barbarians,
    a lot is expected of us, ceremony-wise.
    We rise to that expectation.

Hazard's Optimism

Harnessed and zipped on a bright
October day, having lied to his wife,
Hazard jumps, and the silk spanks
open, and he is falling safely.

This is what for two years now
he has been painting, in a child's palette
—not the plotted landscape that holds dim
below him, but the human figure dangling safe,
guyed to something silky, hanging here,
full of half-remembered instruction
but falling, and safe.

They must have caught and spanked him
like this when he first fell.
He passes it along now, Hazard's vision.
He is in charge of morale in a morbid time.
He calls out to the sky, his voice
the voice of an animal that makes not words
but a happy incorrigible noise, not
of this time. The colors of autumn
are becoming audible through the haze.

It does not matter that the great masters
could see this without flight, while
dull Hazard must be taken up again and dropped.
He sees it. Then he sees himself
as he would look from the canopy above him,
closing safely (if he can remember
what to do) on the Bruegel landscape.
Inside the bug-like goggles, his eyes water.

Music

Loud

The neighbors have a teenaged girl. Below the hill
where Hazard works in an old barn with a stove,
the neighbors' house is throbbing. It doesn't move
visibly, and he can't hear the Rolling Stones, still,
he can feel it throb. Will the decibels do structural harm
to the child's lovely ears, to the brick house,
to the frail culture of Jefferson and Adams,
Hazard and Franz Kline? They will do no good.
He would bring his own stereo to the barn
and make soft counter-seisms of Coltrane or Strauss,
but he can't paint to music, he never could.

ii

The Life of the Artist
in Capitalist Society (c. 1927)

When he was small, one day he was kept indoors
with a cold. His mother was hoovering the rug,
a new liberation then—the neighbors
still had carpet-sweepers. One had a maid
with a dustpan on a stick and a little broom.

Child Hazard sprawled on the hoovered part with the dog,
under the tall victrola. He played
his favorite of the thick black

hooting discs, with fleurs-de-lys stamped on the back,
he played 'The Land of the Sky-Blue Waters' loud.
(To make it loud you opened all four doors
and with just a diaphragm it filled the room.)

When he asked her, 'Mother, how do they get
the lady into the record so she sings?'
his mother said, at least he thinks she said,
over the hoover (who hadn't been president yet)
'When a person sings, they press him in hot wax.'
(She was never much on scientific things.)

Shocked at the death of Jessica Dragonette,
he slipped her black corpse back into one of the books
and thought of the heavy cost an artist paid.
Then he thought how queer it was to own
all those pressed singers and a gramophone
and not to be able to afford a live maid.

Wholesome

Hazard's friend Elliott is homosexual. Prodigious
feats of understanding on both sides. It strikes
Hazard as making a complicated matter
more complicated. Very straightforward
on the contrary, Elliott says, who is forever
kissing Hazard's wife hello and goodbye.

In the gallery at the opening almond-
eyed young men materialize. They look at the pictures
as though they were mirrors. Elliott is better known
than Hazard, perhaps a little fashionable.
He administers cocktails, he drinks wisely.

In all fairness, Hazard tells himself
and, *nothing human is alien to me*
and, *the truth is, a great mind must be androgynous,*
(*Coleridge*). But it doesn't bear dwelling on.

Politics

Tonight Hazard's father and stepmother are having
jazz for McGovern. In the old game-room
the old liberals listen as the quintet builds
crazy houses out of skin and brass, crumbling
the house of decorum, everybody likes that.

For decades they have paid for the refurbishing
of America and they have not got their money's worth.
Now they listen, hopeful,
to the hard rock for McGovern.

The ceiling in this palace needs fixing,
the chalky blue paint is like an old heaven
but there are holes and flaking.
They had movies here when grandpa was solvent.

Hazard desires his wife, the way people
on the trains to the death-camps were seized
by irrational lust. She is the youngest woman
in the room, he would like to be in bed
with her now, he would like to be president.

He has not been to his studio
in four days, he asks the bar-tender,
a college boy with a pony-tail, for more gin.
He stands in the doorway. Forsythia and lilac
have overgrown the porch, there is the rich
smell of wood-rot. What twenty years will do
to untended shrubbery and America and Hazard.

Where
He's Staying
Now

I look out of these two holes, or I run
into the other two and listen. Is Hazard trapped in here?

I have had on this funny suit for years, it's getting
baggy, but I can still move all the parts.

In the top I can make satisfying noises.
I fill it again & again with things I want.
It does not like them all. I empty it furtively.

It is rubbery and durable, I wash it.
People sometimes touch it, that feels good
although I am deep inside.

I do not find it absurd—is this because
I am used to it? (trapped in it? Where are we?
This is certainly not rubber or a cheap plastic.)

If I crawl out of it at night, it comes
snuffling after me and swallows me. It says
it is looking for pictures. I tell it
it has come to the wrong man.

Squire Hazard Walks

i

Near the big spruce, on the path that goes
to the compost heap, broken members
of a blue-jay have been assembled
as if to determine the cause of
a crash without survivors.

                   Walking
with Hazard, the cat does not observe
them. The cat will be disassembled
in his own time by underground technicians.
At this point Hazard's thought turns chicken.
It is the first warm May day, the rich
black compost heap is full of promise.

ii

Ladyslippers,
gypsy plants long
absent, have come
back this cold May.
Erotic, stern
ambiguous
shapes, they can blight
or prosper a
season's footwork
for who finds them.

They choose a dry
road-side oak stand
where nine beer cans
were thrown last fall
by men he had
thought damned (he damned
them) .

      It is with
superstition
now he picks them
up, spilling brown
winter ale from
ladyslippers'
rusty shrines or
garden-houses.
Peace on vandals
and litterers,
crooked gypsies.

iii

Ho the stones came riding here
like hunters, on their ice-barges,
and where they debarked, they stay.

Before this was a place, before
the dusty trees or erect Mercator—
no topsoil, no cerebral hemisphere
that could hold coordinates—stones.
Freeholder Hazard and the bank
hold the place now from them.

Here's one, fern-hatted, big as a mastodon,
from the time when heroes were braggarts,
who would not sell. And underneath there are
vast limbs sprawling northeast-southwest,
the way country people slept so the polar current
would not affect their powers.

Sometimes he digs up sharpened ones,
flints- and quartzes-come-lately,
flown here on the ends of sticks
by hungrier men, wrestled to earth
by rabbit or deer, little stones
who rode to their quiet on flesh-barges.

And what swirling was in residence
here before the ice-sleds unloaded?
What is held in perpetuity? The town hall
with all the records will move off
one day, without legal notice.
The air that's passed through his lungs
or the love through his head and loins
are more his to keep than this boulder-camp,
ready to move off whenever the hunt resumes.

Look at Me!
Look at Me!

Erica is eight, a factory of will.
Sometimes she will home in on Hazard and ride
his knee with an intensity few women
can muster in bed, and when she comes back from
dancing-class, she dances. Then she is not his
wife's daughter but Eve's, then for minutes at a
time they have one another's attention. She
begins and ends these games. She gets what she wants.

Peter is almost ten. His electric trains
(the small kind, the best) provide much of Hazard's
fantasy life. Together they build tunnels
and alps out of wet newspaper and paint them
with tedious realism. There is no longer
a dining-room. Hazard and the boy dispute
schedules reasonably, passenger and freight.
They have little else in common. Each of them
prefers friends his own age and listens to them.
Only household money is withheld by his
wife nowadays, everything else goes for trains.
It seems a roundabout form of discourse.

Hazard's good mother-in-law has got to be
seventy-five. When he surprises her talking
with the children he understands what attention
is. Perhaps only across such years can it
happen disinterestedly. Perhaps that
is why we are vouchsafed three generations—
they are a teaching device. But for whom? How the
old lady (who is so full of energy
no one could think of her that way) watches

and listens, how the children unfold like paper
flowers, watched and listened to.
                                    In his studio
Hazard stares at the vain, self-centered landscape
he's working on now. It is going well. It
revels in his onanistic attention

At intervals he can muster ravenous
attention to gin, dinner, and his mysterious
woman, who has other interests. He calls
himself a painter. He has strong visual
curiosity, he is interested
in things. But he needs a lot of attention
and all four of his grandparents are dead.

His Plans
for Old Age

He disagrees with Simone de Beauvoir
in her civilized Gallic gloom, may she be loved
and beautiful without wrinkles until it takes
carbon dating to determine her age.

He's with Yeats, for adult education—
hand-clapping lessons for the soul,
compulsory singing lessons for the soul,
in his case, tone-deaf.
He agrees with Auden, old people can show
'what grace of spirit can create,'
modeling the flesh when it's no longer flashy.
That's the kind of lift he wants for his jowls,
let grace of spirit tuck up the flesh
under his ears and chin with a bare scalpel,
no anesthetic or anything, let grace of spirit
shape up his skull for afterwards.

Man and artist, he is working on his ways
so that when he becomes set in them
as old people must, for all that their souls
clap hands, for all that their spirits dance,
his ways will have grace, his pictures will have class.

He is founding a sect for the radical old,
freaks you may call them but you're wrong,
who persist in being at home in the world,
who just naturally feel it's a good bind to be in,
let the young feel as uncanny as they like.
Oldbodies, he calls them affectionately

as he towels his own in the morning
in front of the mirror, not getting any flashier.
He thinks about Titian and Renoir a lot
in this connection. Nothing is unseemly
that takes its rise in love. If only his energy lasts.

At the Natural History Museum

Past a swim-by of deep-sea fish,
cold rockets in a tank of air, tamed
by their right names and their Latin underneath,
he walks toward the cafeteria. It grows dark.
October clouds shadow the frosted-glass roof,
the dinosaurs appear, mahogany bones.
The family died out.

On the far wall, a fierce one rears erect,
his shoulders thrown back like a man's
when he is loved or seeks high office.
His jaws are strong pliers. Dawn men watch in awe
from the bushes this blood cousin
in a world of crusty things.

But the family dies out before his eyes,
grass-eaters first, then taloned meat-eaters.
Some of the bones have been fleshed out with plaster
but Hazard and the guard are the oldest living things
here. Even the author of the comic verse
about extinction, copied at the monster's feet,
has gone his bony way.

We descend by chosen cells that are not lost,
though they wander off in streams and rivulets.
Not everyone has issue in this creation.
Cousins-german are everywhere in the shale
and marshes under this dry house. In slime, in sperm,
our living cousins flow.

And grazers or killers, each time we must stoop low
and enter by some thigh-lintel, gentle as rills.
Who consents to his own return, Nietzsche says,
participates in the divinity of the world.
Perhaps I have already eddied on, out of this backwater,
man, on my way to the cafeteria, Hazard thinks.
Perhaps nothing dies but husks.

Rhode Island

Here at the seashore they use the clouds over & over
again, like the rented animals in *Aïda*.
In the late morning the land breeze
turns and now the extras are driving
all the white elephants the other way.
What language are the children shouting in?
He is lying on the beach listening.

The sand knocks like glass, struck by bare heels.
He tries to remember snow noise.
Would powder snow ping like that?
But you don't lie with your ear to powder snow.
Why doesn't the girl who takes care
of the children, a Yale girl without flaw,
know the difference between *lay* and *lie?*

He tries to remember snow, his season.
The mind is in charge of things then.
Summer is for animals, the ocean is erotic,
all that openness and swaying.
No matter how often you make love
in August you're always aware of genitalia,
your own and the half-naked others'.
Even with the gracefulest bathers
you're aware of their kinship with porpoises,
mammals disporting themselves in a blue element,
smelling slightly of fish. Porpoise Hazard
watches himself awhile, like a blue movie.

In the other hemisphere now people
are standing up, at work at their easels.
There they think about love at night
when they take off their serious clothes
and go to bed sandlessly, under blankets.

Today the children, his own among them,
are apparently shouting fluently in Portuguese,
using the colonial dialect of Brazil.
It is just as well, they have all been changed
into small shrill marginal animals,
he would not want to understand them again
until after Labor Day. He just lays there.

The Ghosts
of the House

Enabling love, roof of this drafty hutch
of children and friends and pets, and chiefly of the dear
one asleep beside me now, the warm body-house
I sack like a hun nightly in your service,
take care of the haunts who stay with us here.

In a little space for a long while they've walked,
wakeful when we sleep, averting their sad glance
when we're clumsy with one another, they look
at something we can't look at yet, they creak the boards
beside the bed we creak, in some hard durance.

And if we're weary at night, what must they be?
Bed them like us at last under your roof.
You who have sternly set all lovers to walk
the hallways of the world-hutch for a lucky while,
speaking good of our short durance here,

wishing our sibling spirits nothing but good,
let them see these chambers once with the daylight eyes
you lend to lovers for our mortal time.
Or change some loveless stalker into me
before my bone-house clatters into lime.

Nausea

In the courtyard of the Brera,
the great gallery in Milan
(he isn't dropping place-names,
that's simply where it happened),
a sparrow chased a butterfly
around the sunny oblong
for what must have seemed forever
to an insect or a bird—
it was long enough for Hazard.

Above an enormous statue
of Napoleon buck-naked
they turned and wove like pilots
in a dog-fight (he was always
scared shitless in the Navy
when they had to practice dog-fights—
once he threw up in the cockpit).
This butterfly was agile,
he could really wrap it up,
turning in half the circle
of the fat city bird.
Climbing nimblier than the sparrow,
he did fishtails and chandelles,
trying to stall him out.
Over Normandy or London
or the carriers at Leyte
the insect would have won.
Like David with Goliath
(thought lightly-bibled Hazard)
the plucky lepidopteran
would slay the gross-beaked monster

with feathers sleek as Satan's
and metal eyes and claws.

But that's not how it was.
Chomp, and the greedy sparrow
was off behind a column
on the balcony above them
with the emblem of the soul.
Before his wife could lure him
inside to see the Piero
and the unique Mantegnas
(the *pictures,* for god's sake)
he had a fearful vision,
a memory it was, really:
in a cockpit full of chili
with cold terror in his gut
he flies round and round and round
a blue oblong in Texas,
trying to escape his friend.

Nixon's
the One

November 8, a cold rain. Hazard discovered
on the blacktop driveway, trying to get the McGovern-
Shriver stickers off his '65 Ford.
The one on the back bumper is already faded,
the red so bleached it could be declaring
Madly for Adlai. It's gummy, it tears.
The two on his wife's car, a new VW
kept dry in the garage, came off easily.
(In August somebody said the VW's
must be coming off the line in Stuttgart
with McGovern-Shriver stickers.
But Nader was right: in collision
with a fat American machine they're murder.

Our battlefields are accidents, too,
human errors like this late one:
we elect to murder, we murder to elect.)

Who were all those cheering on the gray glass
screen last night, loving their violent darling,
America, whom they had married to money?
He couldn't tarry at that feast—when the wine
ran out, they would change blood to money.

Even in the slanting rain, Hazard is aware
of his oilskin comfort. He is comfortably off,
a two-car man. Somewhere he has gotten out of touch.
This morning he is alone in the defoliated

landscape (oh, his family is indoors there,
snug, adapting to the political weather),
the patrol he scouted with, wiped out.
Standing now on the asphalt no-man's-land,
his hands bloodied with patriotic mucilage,
he cannot shake his unpopular conviction
that his nation has bitterly misspoken itself.

February 14

(Valerie Hazard finds on her desk a strange self-portrait
by her husband and a note which she takes to be a valentine
and on the whole well-meant.)

What you have given me,
in those long moments when our words
come back, our breaths come back,
is a whole man at last,
and keeping me, remembers:

On deck one night, the moon past full
coming up over the planet's edge,
the big globe rippling its skin,
the smaller already accepting its waning
and talking about vast skiey distances.
I had not met you yet.
Aft, the aircraft folded like mantises,
ahead and abeam, destroyers running like hounds,
and the wind.

A sentry walked off
the rolled front of the flight deck,
crying *oh* as he fell to the sea.
Lost in the cold skin of the globe,
he cried *oh* for less than, panted
for less than love, going away,
the loneliest noise that ever wound in my ear.

I think dear one that one day I'll fall off
this galaxy, leaving husk and canvas behind,
the loneliness I'll take with me made whole,
myself made whole, by what we've said
in these knocking moments, oh,
and keeping, as hearts keep,
(husk and canvas being little abandoned houses)
and going away so.

Winter:
He Shapes Up

Now autumn has finished scolding
with sumac, sun and jays
his heavy-lidded ways,
his drinking and his balding.

Today the first snow fell.
It hung in the hollow air
making space tangible,
showing him how things are.

He watches the yellow larches
guttering on their boles
like half-extinguished torches
as the planet tilts and cools

and the laurel understory
that shields the hill from harm
—the merest rag of glory
will keep ambition warm.

Gnawed by a vision of rightness
that no one else seems to see,
what can a man do
but bear witness?

And what has he got to tell?
Only the shaped things he's seen—
a few things made by men,
a galaxy made well.

Though more of each day is dark,
though he's awkward at the job,
he squeezes paint from a tube.
Hazard is back at work.

A Note About the Author

William Meredith was born in New York City in 1919, was
graduated from Princeton in 1940, and served as a naval
aviator during the Second World War. His first book of
poems, *Love Letter from an Impossible Land,* was chosen by
Archibald MacLeish, in 1944, for the Yale Series of Younger
Poets; the title poem had been written the year before, in
the Aleutian Islands. *Ships and Other Figures,* his second
book of verse, was published in Princeton in 1948, and *The
Open Sea* and *The Wreck of the Thresher* in 1958 and 1964
respectively, both by Knopf. *Earth Walk: New & Selected
Poems* (Knopf 1970) draws on all of his earlier books
of verse.

William Meredith has won three of *Poetry*'s annual prizes,
and a grant and the Loines Award from the National
Academy of Arts and Letters, of which he became a member
in 1968. Since 1964 he has been a chancellor of the Academy
of American Poets. Mr. Meredith has taught at Princeton,
the University of Hawaii, Middlebury College, Breadloaf,
and Carnegie-Mellon University, but has been primarily
associated with Connecticut College since 1955.

A Note on the Type

This book was set in a type face called Bulmer. This dis-
tinguished letter is a replica of a type long famous in the
history of English printing that was designed and cut by
William Martin about 1790 for William Bulmer of the Shake-
speare Press. In design, it is all but a modern face, with
vertical stress, sharp differentiation between the thick and
thin strokes, and nearly flat serifs. The decorative italic
shows the influence of Baskerville; Martin was John Baskerville's
pupil.
The book was designed by Betty Anderson and was composed,
printed, and bound by Kingsport Press, Inc., Kingsport,
Tennessee.